99
wl-ch

D0842690

APR   2005

What did the ancient Greeks wear? What did they do for fun? When were the very first Olympics held? How are our modern Olympics similar to the ancient Olympics?

Find out the answers to these questions and more in . . .

**Magic Tree House®
Research Guide**

ANCIENT GREECE
AND THE OLYMPICS

A nonfiction companion to
Hour of the Olympics

It's Jack and Annie's very own guide to the fascinating ancient Greeks and the first Olympic Games!

Including:
• Greek myths
• Famous ancient Greeks
• Amazing early Olympic events
• The Olympic Games today
And much more!

Here's what people are saying
about the Magic Tree House®
Research Guides:

*Your Research Guides are a great addition
to the Magic Tree House series! I have used*
Rain Forests *and* Space *as "read-alouds"
during science units. Thank you!*—Cheryl
M., teacher

*My eight-year-old son thinks your books are
great—and I agree. I wish my high school
students had read the Research Guides when
they were his age.*—John F., parent and
teacher

*My son loves the Research Guides. He has
even asked for a notebook, which he takes
with him to the museum for his research.*
—A parent

*I love your books. I have a great library at
home filled with your books and Research
Guides. The* [Knights and Castles] *Research
Guide really helped me do a report on castles
and knights!*—A young reader

Magic Tree House®
Research Guide

ANCIENT GREECE
AND THE OLYMPICS

A nonfiction companion to
Hour of the Olympics

by Mary Pope Osborne
and Natalie Pope Boyce

illustrated by Sal Murdocca

A STEPPING STONE BOOK™
Random House ⌂ New York

www.randomhouse.com/magictreehouse

Library of Congress Cataloging-in-Publication Data
Osborne, Mary Pope.
Ancient Greece and the Olympics : a nonfiction companion to
Hour of the Olympics / by Mary Pope Osborne and Natalie Pope Boyce ;
illustrated by Sal Murdocca.
    p. cm. — (Magic tree house research guide) "A stepping stone book."
SUMMARY: Annie and Jack present information about ancient Greece and the
athletic events known as the Olympic Games that were held there.
ISBN 0-375-82378-6 (trade) — ISBN 0-375-92378-0 (lib. bdg.)
1. Olympic games (Ancient)—Juvenile literature. [1. Olympic games
(Ancient). 2. Greece—History—To 146 B.C.] I. Boyce, Natalie Pope.
II. Murdocca, Sal, ill. III. Osborne, Mary Pope. Hour of the Olympics.
IV. Title. V. Series.
GV23.O73 2004   796.48—dc22   2003013090

Printed in the United States of America   First Edition
10 9 8 7 6 5 4 3 2

For Bill Kruse

Scientific Consultant:
DR. MIKE NORRIS, Associate Museum Educator, The Metropolitan Museum of Art, New York, New York.

Very special thanks to Will Osborne, for his invaluable encouragement and help.

We would also like to acknowledge Pam Kosty and the staff at the University of Pennsylvania Museum of Archaeology and Anthropology; Paul Coughlin for his ongoing photographic contribution to the series; and, as always, the great creative team at Random House: Joanne Yates, Angela Roberts, Cathy Goldsmith, Mallory Loehr, and especially our editor, Shana Corey, whose patience, skill, and diligence made this book possible.

ANCIENT GREECE
AND THE OLYMPICS

Contents

Dear Readers,

The great thing about learning is that it never stops! And best of all, it can be a lot of fun.

Our adventures in <u>Hour of the Olympics</u> taught us a lot about ancient Greece. But we wanted to learn more. We wanted to find out how the ancient Greeks lived. And we really wanted to know about the ancient Olympics. We wondered if the Games were as popular as they are now. Guess what? We found out they were!

First we went to the library. There were lots of books there on ancient Greece. The books had great pictures. We could imagine

the people who lived then. It was harder to find information on the ancient Olympics. This is where the Internet came in handy. We found some good sites that really helped. And finally, we visited a museum that had many things from ancient Greece.

When we finished our research, we knew a lot. Now we're going to share it with you. Get out your notebooks. Get ready! We're traveling back over 2,000 years. It's time to meet the ancient Greeks!

Jack

Annie

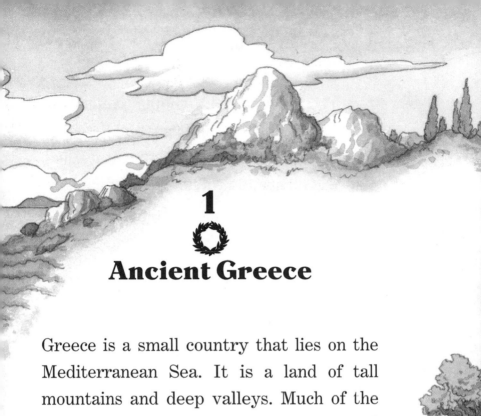

1

Ancient Greece

Greece is a small country that lies on the Mediterranean Sea. It is a land of tall mountains and deep valleys. Much of the soil is dry and rocky. Olive groves and grapevines dot the hillsides.

People first settled in Greece thousands of years ago. They were simple shepherds, farmers, and fishermen. As the years passed, the country changed. Greeks lived in cities as well as in the country.

The ancient (AIN-shunt) Greeks became great artists, writers, builders, and thinkers. By 500 BC, Greek culture had spread all around the Mediterranean and Black seas.

Athens

Ancient Greece was divided into about 300 city-states, or *poleis* (POE-lace). A city-state was made up of a city and the countryside around it. The city governed the city-state. Athens was one of the most powerful city-states. It got its name from Athena, the goddess of wisdom.

Athens was a center of art and learning. The people who lived in Athens were called Athenians (uh-THEE-nee-unz). Athenians loved beauty. They built great buildings. They created wonderful

Ruins of ancient Athens

art. They wrote poetry and plays. They studied math and science.

Athens had one of the first democratic (dem-uh-KRA-tick) governments in the world. This means that the people, not a king, ran the government.

Voting was very important in ancient Greek democracy. In Athens, only male citizens (SIT-uh-zunz) 20 years old or older could vote. A citizen was usually some-one born in Athens. Women could not vote. Slaves could not be citizens and had no voting rights.

Voters

20 years old or older

Citizens

Men only

No slaves

Sparta

Sparta was a powerful rival (RIE-vul) of Athens. Sparta and Athens often fought one another. But sometimes they joined together to fight other countries.

Sparta was not a democracy like Athens. It was ruled by two kings.

Spartans were warriors. They spent

much of their time training for war. They didn't share the Athenians' love of beauty and learning. They left behind no beautiful buildings or art.

Greek soldiers sometimes rode into battle on elephants.

This helmet was worn by an ancient Greek warrior around 600 BC.

Athens and Sparta were very different. But even though the city-states were not all alike, they had many things in common. Everyone spoke Greek. They worshiped the same gods. They had many of the same customs. And they were all proud to call themselves Greek.

17

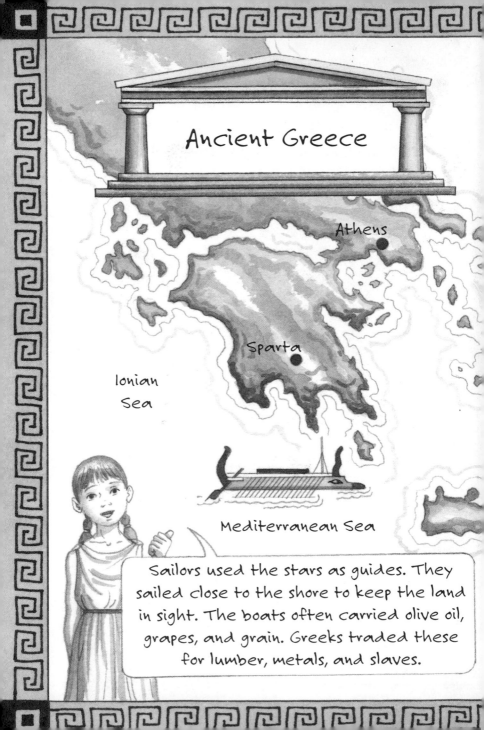

Ancient Greece

Athens

Sparta

Ionian
Sea

Mediterranean Sea

Sailors used the stars as guides. They sailed close to the shore to keep the land in sight. The boats often carried olive oil, grapes, and grain. Greeks traded these for lumber, metals, and slaves.

Most cities in Greece were near the Mediterranean Sea. There were few roads. Traveling by boat was usually easier than traveling over the hilly land.

Aegean Sea

Persian Empire

Rhodes

Crete

Greeks sailed around the Mediterranean on small boats. The boats were made of wood. Some had only one sail. Other boats were rowed with oars.

2

Religion

Religion was a big part of Greek life. Greeks worshiped many different gods. They imagined the gods looked and acted like humans with special powers. They told stories about the gods' adventures. These stories were called *myths*.

The Greeks believed there were 12 major gods. They thought these gods lived on top of the tallest mountain in Greece. It was called Olympus (oh-LIM-pus). The

Greeks believed the gods lived happy lives on Olympus. Everyone thought they rested all day and ate wonderful food called *ambrosia* (am-BRO-zhuh).

Religion
12 major gods
Lived good life on Mount Olympus
Ate ambrosia

People believed the gods punished them when they were angry. To please the gods, people honored them with gifts and prayers. Families often had altars in the house. They prayed to their favorite gods for protection.

Temples
The Greeks built temples for the gods. Temples were often the largest buildings in

ancient Greece. Many were very beautiful. Each temple had a statue of a god inside. Some temple statues were 40 feet tall. That's as tall as a school bus standing on end! Sometimes the statues were covered with gold and ivory.

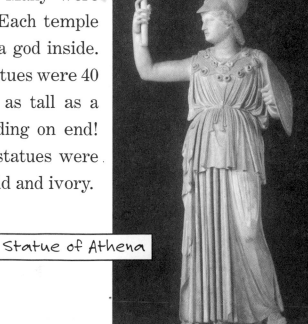

Statue of Athena

Festivals

The Greeks held festivals to honor the gods. A festival was an exciting event.

People often traveled to the festival from miles away. They walked to the temple in lines called *processions* (pruh-SEH-shunz). They brought food, animals, and other gifts to offer the gods.

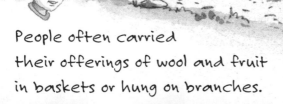

People often carried their offerings of wool and fruit in baskets or hung on branches.

When they arrived, they sometimes washed the temple statue. Then they put new clothes on it.

Festivals often included sporting events. Greeks believed sports honored the gods. People also danced and made music. They believed all these things made the gods happy.

Turn the page to meet some of our favorite gods.

Zeus

(zoose)

Zeus was ruler of the gods. He was god of the sky, clouds, and rain. When Zeus was angry, he hurled thunder and bolts of lightning down to earth. Zeus rewarded people who pleased him. But if someone made him mad, watch out! One of Zeus's enemies was named Atlas (AT-lus). Zeus made Atlas hold up the sky on his back forever!

Atlas is also the name for a book of maps.

Zeus's wife was Hera (HEH-ruh), but he fell in love with many other women. He always tried to hide his other loves from Hera. The Greeks believed that when the oak leaves rustled, Zeus was talking.

Hera

(HEH-ruh)

Hera was the goddess of marriage and married women. She was very jealous of Zeus's girlfriends. Their fights made the heavens shake!

Hera never forgave the women Zeus fell in love with. She spent all her time getting even with them. One time Hera was looking for Zeus. She thought he was with his girlfriends. She was distracted by a beautiful girl named Echo. Echo was laughing and chattering. As Echo talked, the girls managed to slip away.

Our word echo comes from this myth!

Hera got very angry at Echo. She forbade her ever to speak her own thoughts. Instead, poor Echo could only repeat the last word someone said to her over and over again.

Poseidon

(poe-SIDE-un)

Zeus had a brother named Poseidon. He was god of the seas. Poseidon lived in a palace under the sea. He always carried a

trident (TRY-dent). When he was angry, he would hit the water with it. This caused terrible earthquakes, storms, and drownings.

A <u>trident</u> is a three-pronged spear.

In one myth, Poseidon got angry when the Greeks lost a war. The soldiers tried to return to Greece on ships. Poseidon sent a huge storm over the ocean. The storm wrecked all the ships.

Sailors always thanked Poseidon when the seas were calm.

Aphrodite

(af-ruh-DIE-tee)

Aphrodite was the goddess of love and beauty. Some myths said she came from foam in the sea.

Aphros means "foam" in Greek.

Aphrodite was so charming that no one could resist her. Flowers sprang up when she walked through the fields. The waves laughed when she passed by.

Aphrodite is always shown with a smiling face. But she caused problems among the gods, too. She made them fall in love with her when they shouldn't.

Her special bird was the dove, and her tree was the myrtle.

Athena

(uh-THEEN-uh)

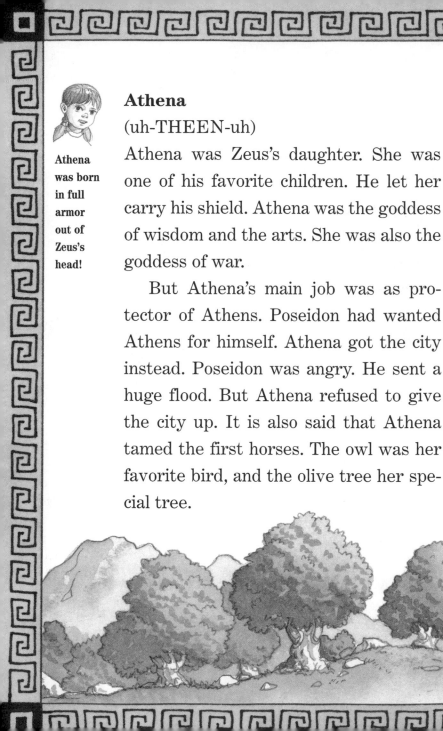

Athena was born in full armor out of Zeus's head!

Athena was Zeus's daughter. She was one of his favorite children. He let her carry his shield. Athena was the goddess of wisdom and the arts. She was also the goddess of war.

But Athena's main job was as protector of Athens. Poseidon had wanted Athens for himself. Athena got the city instead. Poseidon was angry. He sent a huge flood. But Athena refused to give the city up. It is also said that Athena tamed the first horses. The owl was her favorite bird, and the olive tree her special tree.

Phoebus Apollo

(FEE-bus uh-PAHL-oh)

Zeus was also the father of Phoebus Apollo. *Phoebus* means "shining and bright" in Greek. Phoebus Apollo was usually just called Apollo.

Apollo was a beautiful god with shining golden hair. He was the god of the sun, healing, music, and poetry.

Apollo carried a silver bow and raced his chariot across the sky. He often played music for the gods on his golden lyre.

A lyre is a harp-like instrument.

The dolphin, wolf, swan, and crow were Apollo's favorite animals. The laurel was his special tree.

3

Daily Life in Ancient Greece

Greek cities were usually protected by walls. The walled section of Athens was called the Acropolis (uh-CROP-uh-lis). It stood on a hill overlooking the city. People did not live on the Acropolis. They lived in houses and apartments in the city below.

Agora comes
from a Greek
word that
means
"to come
together."

Much of daily life in Athens and ancient Greece took place in the *agora* (AG-ur-uh). The agora was the marketplace. It was crowded with stalls selling food, crafts, and other household items. In Athens, men usually did all the shopping. They often met in the agora to visit and chat about the news of the day. There were also important public buildings, temples, and houses in the agora.

40

People came from all over to sell their goods in the agora.

Houses

Greek houses and apartment buildings were made of stone, clay, or wood. The roofs were made of tile or reeds.

Inside there were usually very few rooms. The floors were made of packed dirt or stone. There were wooden chairs, tables, and couches. The family stored their things in baskets or chests.

Couches were often for sleeping as well as sitting.

In the middle of the house stood an open courtyard. In good weather, the family gathered there to relax.

Sometimes the family cooked and ate their meals in the courtyard. They often ate bread, olive oil, goat cheese, and a porridge made of grains. They also ate figs, grapes, and honey.

Tile roof

Women spent most of their time in the house. When they left, a female slave went with them.

Kitchen

Bedroom

Girls and women used a belt to shorten their tunics when they exercised.

Clothing and Grooming

Greek clothes were very simple. Everyone wore a rectangular piece of cloth called a *tunic* (TOO-nick). Men wore tunics called *chitons* (KIE-tunz) that came to the knee. Women and girls wore a longer tunic called a *peplos* (PEP-lus).

Woman wearing <u>peplos</u>

Greek men and women used scented oils in their hair.

Greeks often went barefoot at home. At other times, they wore sandals, slippers, or boots.

Dress like an ancient Greek!

1. Get an old sheet.
2. Fold it in half.
3. Wrap it around your body.
4. Pin it at the shoulders.
5. Tie a belt around your waist.
6. Don't trip!

Help! Lead is poisonous!

Rich women wore jewelry and make-up. Sometimes they put white powdered lead on their faces to look pale. Men often went to barbershops to get their hair cut and to see their friends. One Greek man wrote that barbershops were like "parties without wine."

This ancient Greek painting shows a woman looking at herself in a polished-bronze mirror.

Education

Schools in ancient Greece were just for boys. In Athens, boys began school when they were seven years old. The boys learned reading, writing, and poetry. They also studied music and sports. Sports were very important in ancient Greece. The Greeks believed in a strong mind in a healthy body.

Slaves sometimes went to school with boys to make them behave!

47

In Athens, girls stayed at home and learned how to run a house. Most mothers taught their daughters to spin, weave, sew, and cook. If a girl was rich, she usually learned to read and to write at home.

The two women on the right are preparing wool to make cloth.

Spartan boys went away to military schools when they were seven years old. Their schools taught them how to be soldiers.

In Sparta, girls had more freedom than in Athens. Although they didn't go to school, they learned sports, singing, and dancing. Their main job was to grow up and produce strong Spartan boys!

Marriage

Greek girls and women seldom met men who were not in their family. When male visitors arrived, women and girls went into a separate room. But girls in Athens married very young. They were usually only 15 years old!

Their fathers chose their husbands. The men were often in their thirties.

49

Before marriage, girls presented all their toys to the goddess Artemis (AR-tuh-mis). This meant that childhood had come to an end.

Fun

Ancient Greeks did many things for fun. Some children enjoyed board games that were almost like checkers and chess.

These figures show people playing a popular ancient Greek game called knucklebones.

Greek boys and girls played with hoops and dolls. They also played with animals made out of clay or wood.

Children kept pets like birds, dogs, mice, turtles, and goats.

Greeks often danced and played music. They had a lot of different dances. There were dances to honor the gods. There were dances for weddings and for funerals. There were also dances for harvest time and for victory in war.

Shepherds even played music to their sheep.

Gymnasium comes from a Greek word that means "to exercise naked"! Yikes!

During the day, boys and men spent time at the *gymnasium* (jim-NAY-zee-um). The gymnasium was like a park where people went to play sports and exercised.

In the evening, men sometimes gave parties called *symposia* (sim-POE-zee-uh). These parties were for men only. Except for slave girls, women and girls were not allowed. Servants met guests at the door and washed their feet.

Everyone drank wine, ate, and talked. Sometimes they recited poetry and sang.

During parties, men lay on couches. Sometimes they wore flowers in their hair.

The ancient Greeks had busy lives. They enjoyed their family and their friends. They liked parties, music, and dance. Like people today, they spent time playing sports and keeping fit. But for many Greeks, at the very center of life was a love of learning and beauty.

Olive Trees

Olive trees grow well in the dry, rocky soil of Greece. The ancient Greeks believed Athena gave the first olive trees to Athens. Over the years, they became very important to ancient Greece.

Olive trees are very strong. They can survive heavy winds and dry weather. The Greeks believed they were symbols of strength and peace. In some city-states, it was a serious crime to cut one down!

The Greeks cleaned their skin with olive oil and used it on their hair.

One Greek poet called olive oil "liquid gold."

4

The Culture
of Ancient Greece

Ancient Greece is famous for its *culture*
(KUL-chur). Culture is the way a group of
people think and live and the art they cre-
ate. Many Greeks were great thinkers,
writers, artists, and builders. Others made
discoveries in science and medicine. The
ideas and works of ancient Greece still in-
spire us today.

Philosopher means "lover of wisdom" in Greek.

Philosophy

Some of the best thinkers in Greece were the *philosophers* (fil-AHS-uh-furz). Philosophers were people who loved wisdom and learning. They were often teachers.

Socrates (SOCK-ruh-teez) was one of the greatest philosophers. He taught people how best to live their lives. Socrates believed that money was not enough to make a person happy. He believed that a good person was a happy person.

Socrates did not leave any writing behind. But his student Plato (PLAY-toe) wrote down what Socrates said. Plato also became a famous philosopher. He ran a school called the Academy (uh-KA-duh-mee).

Science and Medicine

The Greeks learned a lot about science and medicine. Greek scientists decided that facts, not myths, explained the way things worked. They studied things like the tides and the stars. Some scientists even figured out how to predict an eclipse. Others believed the earth was round, not flat.

Most Greeks thought the earth was the center of the universe. Wrong!

Greek doctors studied the human body to learn how it worked. One famous Greek doctor was named Hippocrates (hip-POCK-ruh-teez). He wrote an *oath* for doctors. An oath is a strong prom-ise. Ancient

Hippocrates

Greek doctors used herbs and other plants as medicine.

Greek doctors promised to do no harm. Doctors still take this oath today. It is called the Hippocratic oath.

Greek Architecture

Greek *architects* (AR-kuh-tekts) built incredible buildings. An architect is someone who designs buildings. The *Parthenon* (PAR-thuh-non) on the Acropolis was one

Parthenon in Athens

of the greatest buildings ever built. It was
the temple of Athena.

Lincoln Memorial in
Washington, D.C.

If you think you've seen buildings built like the Parthenon, you are right!

If you think you saw them in Washington, D.C., you are right again!

Drama

Greeks wrote some of the world's best plays. Drama was popular in ancient Greece. People usually went to plays at festivals. The best writers competed to have their plays performed.

Greeks built the first outdoor theaters. These were called *amphitheaters* (AM-fuh-thee-uh-turz). They were built in a half

Theater at Epidaurus

Some theaters like this one could seat up to 14,000 people.

circle on the slope of a hill. The seats rose up the hill so everyone could see.

The actors were always men. A group of people stood at the front of the stage. They were called the *chorus* (KOR-us). The chorus sang. It also told the audience what was happening.

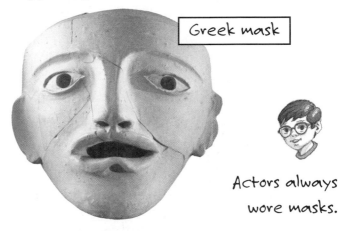

Greek mask

Actors always wore masks.

Poetry

Most Greeks enjoyed reciting poetry. Homer was one of their greatest poets. He wrote over 2,700 years ago.

Homer wrote two famous, long poems. One was *The Iliad* (IL-ee-ud). It was about a war between the Greeks and the Trojans (TRO-junz).

Another is called *The Odyssey* (OD-

Homer

uh-see). It is about the adventures of a hero named Odysseus (oh-DIS-ee-us). You can find these poems in libraries and bookstores today.

Arts

Greeks were great artists and craftsmen. In Athens, sculptors had workshops all over the city. They created beautiful statues of bronze and marble.

Greek potters made wonderful pottery. The decoration on many Athenian pots and vases shows scenes of heroes. Others show us how people looked and lived.

The ancient Greeks left a rich culture. We still read the writings and see the plays of ancient Greece. We still study their philosophers. We still admire their art and architecture. The ancient Greeks left gifts for the whole world to enjoy.

Turn the page to learn how to speak Greek!

Speak Greek!

English

Anchor
Bible
Climate
Democracy
Drama
Hero
Museum
Olympics
School
Theater
Zone

English has a lot of words that come from ancient Greece. In fact, the word *alphabet* comes from the first two letters of the Greek alphabet . . . *alpha* and *beta*. You probably know more Greek than you think!

Greek

Aykura
Biblia
Klima
Demokratia
Drama
Heros
Mouseion
Olympikos
Schole
Theatron
Zone

Yikes! In the earliest Olympics, athletes wore tunics. Later, they competed without clothes.

5

Early Olympics

The ancient Greeks believed that strong bodies and sports pleased the gods. So they honored the gods with sporting events and contests. The Olympics began as a festival to honor Zeus.

The first Olympics were held in 776 BC. They were held in Olympia in the city-state of Elis. The early Olympics were very simple. There was only one event. Runners ran a footrace called the *stade*.

We get the word <u>stadium</u> from the Greek word <u>stade</u>.

Over the years, other sports were added. People traveled from all over to see the Games. The Olympics became the most popular festival in Greece.

Messengers

The Olympics were held every four years. They lasted five days. The Games were always held during the hottest months of the summer. As the time drew near, messengers left Elis. They traveled all over Greece. It was their job to announce the dates for the Games.

The messengers were easy to spot. They wore cloaks and carried wands!

Who Could Compete?

Only Greek citizens could compete in the Olympics. No one who had committed a crime could compete. Women and slaves were not allowed to be in the Games.

Each city-state chose its best athletes to send to the Olympics. They came from all over Greece.

Some were simple shepherds or fishermen. Others were powerful generals or businessmen. Their skill in sports made them all equal at the Games.

Athlete comes from a Greek word that means "to compete for a prize."

First Olympics
Held in Olympia
Festival for Zeus
Greek citizens
No criminals
No girls or slaves

Kallipateira

There was one woman who didn't obey the rules. Her name was Kallipateira (kahl-ee-PAH-tur-uh). Her father and brother were Olympic winners. After her husband died, she trained her son for the Olympics.

Kallipateira dressed up like a man to

watch him compete. She walked boldly into the stadium. When her son won, she leapt over a barrier to congratulate him. Her clothes got tangled. They came loose. It became clear she was not a man! But Kallipateira was lucky. Because she was from a famous family, she wasn't punished.

The Olympic Truce

There were a lot of wars in ancient Greece. City-states fought each other. They also fought other countries. In order to hold the Olympics, all wars had to stop. A *truce* (troose) was called. A *truce* means no fighting!

These were the rules of the Olympic truce:

1. All wars must stop for three months during Olympic training and the Games.

2. Armies and men with weapons cannot enter the Olympic grounds.

3. There is no death penalty during the Olympics.

4. Athletes can pass safely through any city-state on their way to the Games.

Training

Athletes trained nine months at home before the Olympics began. They trained with coaches. Their coaches carried long sticks. They used them to point out the correct muscles to use. Some trainers liked their athletes to practice to flute music. They felt it gave them rhythm and grace.

This Greek vase shows a trainer with a stick.

As the Olympics drew near, athletes and their trainers began the long journey to Olympia. Some went by boat; others walked or rode horses.

Arrival at Elis

Elis was a town in the city-state of Elis!

After their journey, the athletes arrived at the town of Elis, near Olympia. This was their training ground for another month before the Games.

Ten men met the athletes in Elis. They were the Olympic judges. They wore purple cloaks. They had laurel wreaths on their heads. The judges made sure the athletes obeyed the rules. They divided the athletes into age groups. Athletes usually competed with people in their own age groups.

If anyone cheated, he was punished with a fine or a beating.

Then the athletes had to sand and

weed the tracks before they could practice!

Two days before the Games began, the athletes, coaches, and judges left for Olympia in a great procession.

Turn the page to see how you would train in ancient Greece.

This way

Train like the ancient Greeks!

1. Get someone to play the flute while you exercise.

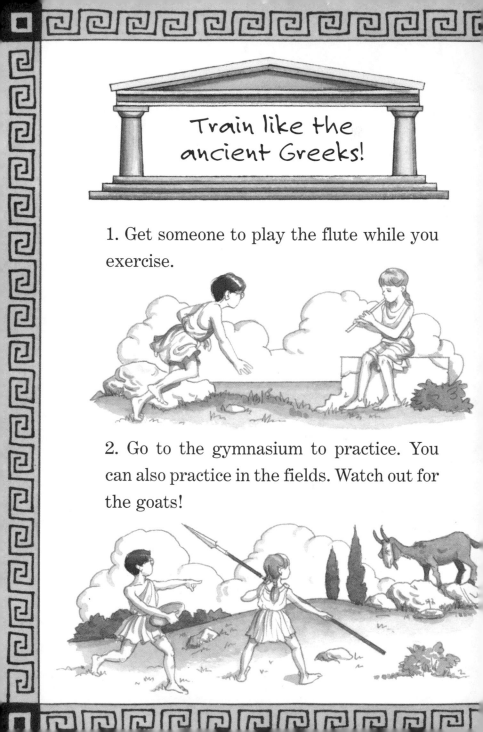

2. Go to the gymnasium to practice. You can also practice in the fields. Watch out for the goats!

3. If you need quick energy, eat grapes, figs, honey, or goat cheese.

4. Be the best sport you can be!

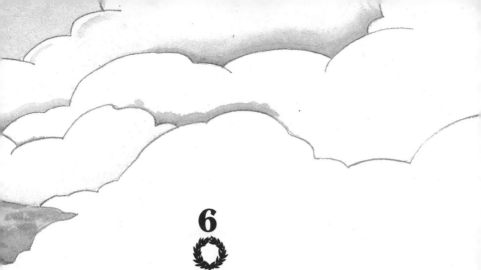

6

Olympic Grounds

As the athletes strode into Olympia, thousands of people lined up to cheer. They had come from all over Greece.

As many as 50,000 people attended the Olympics.

There were tents all over the Olympic grounds. Most visitors and athletes slept in small tents. But rich visitors had huge, fancy ones. They gave dinner parties and entertained their friends inside.

Plato visited the Games when he was 70 years old!

There were plenty of things for everyone to do. People greeted old friends and visited the food stalls. There was music and dancing. Philosophers gave talks. People crowded around as poets read their latest poems.

The Altis

The *Altis* (AL-tus) was one of the most important places in Olympia. It was a special grove of trees in the middle of the grounds.

The temples of Zeus and Hera were there. There were many shrines and altars as well. People visited the Altis to pray and to offer sacrifices.

The third night of the Olympics was always on a full moon. That night, everyone walked in a procession to the temple of Zeus. When they arrived, they offered prayers and sacrifices. During some Olympics, 100 oxen were sacrificed!

Turn the page to read about the amazing statue of Zeus.

The Statue of Zeus

Huge crowds visited the temple of Zeus. They gazed in awe at the great statue of him.

The sculptor Phidias (FID-ee-us) had created a huge Zeus sitting on a throne. One ancient Greek wrote that if Zeus could stand, his head would poke through the ceiling! Zeus's body was covered in ivory and gold.

The statue filled people with wonder. In fact, it is called one of the Seven Wonders of the Ancient World!

The temple was later destroyed by earthquakes and war. Today nothing remains of the temple but scattered ruins.

Ruins of Phidias's workshop

7

Let the Games Begin!

On the first day of the Olympics, athletes and judges took an oath. The athletes and judges stood in front of a statue of Zeus. The athletes swore they had trained for ten months. They also promised to obey the rules. The judges swore to judge the Games fairly.

This statue was called Zeus of the Oaths.

Then there were contests to choose the best trumpet players and *heralds* (HEH-ruldz). Heralds were men who announced the winners. Trumpets blew to alert people that an event was about to begin.

Running

Runners put their feet into long stone grooves. This kept them from taking off too soon.

As trumpets sounded out, runners gathered at the starting line. All the runners had to start at exactly the same time. If a runner started early, he was beaten or forced to leave the Games!

There were several kinds of races. One was the *stade*. The runners sprinted one length of the stadium. The second race was the *diaulos* (die-OW-lus), which was two stadium lengths. The longest race was the *dolichos* (DOE-lick-us), which was a long-distance race. Racers ran 12 lengths of the stadium!

The most difficult race was one in full armor. Runners wore bronze helmets

Runners were forbidden to cast magic spells!

and carried heavy wooden or bronze shields. They looked awkward and funny. The crowds cheered and laughed as the racers lumbered by.

Javelin

The *javelin* (JAV-lin) was used in hunting and in war. It was a long wooden spear as tall as a man. One end was pointed. Throwers held on to a leather strap wound around the javelin. When they threw the javelin, the strap unwound. This made it fly straighter. Whoever threw it farthest won the contest.

Discus

The *discus* (DIS-kus) was shaped like a Frisbee. It could be made of lead, iron, bronze, or even marble. It usually weighed about five and a half pounds.

Athletes held the discus in one hand. Then they tossed it as far as they could. The judges measured the distance to see who threw the farthest.

Long Jump

The long jump began as part of military training. Soldiers often practiced jumping over things.

Flute music played during the long jump.

In the Olympics, the long jump took place on a sand track. Athletes put weights in both hands. They swung their arms forward and then back. Then they jumped as far as they could.

Wrestling

Wrestling also began with soldiers. They practiced it for hand-to-hand combat. Olympic wrestlers wrestled in the sand. In one event, they had to throw another wrestler to the ground from a standing position.

Wrestlers weren't allowed to bite!

Three falls cost wrestlers the match. If their shoulders, backs, chests, or stomachs just barely touched the ground, it was called a fall. Wrestlers put powder and olive oil on their bodies. The oil picked up sand when their bodies touched it. This helped the judges tell if the wrestler really had a fall.

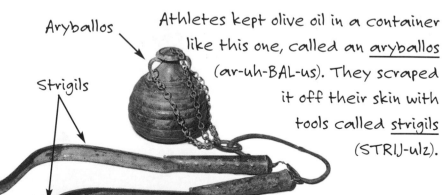

Aryballos

Strigils

Athletes kept olive oil in a container like this one, called an <u>aryballos</u> (ar-uh-BAL-us). They scraped it off their skin with tools called <u>strigils</u> (STRIJ-ulz).

The Pentathlon

The *pentathlon* (pen-TATH-lon) was actually five different events. Each athlete had to be skilled in all five. They were the long jump, the discus, the javelin, running, and wrestling.

Boxing

Boxing was a popular sport. Boxers usually didn't hit below the belt. Instead, they aimed for the head. Good boxers tried to get the other boxer to face the sun. The light made it harder to see.

Danger! Don't try to box like the Greeks!

These boxers are tying on gloves made of leather straps.

Pankration

The *pankration* (pan-KRA-tee-on) was a brutal sport. The name comes from a Greek word that means "all power."

The pankration was a combination of boxing and wrestling. There were not many rules. Boxers could pull hair and kick. They could put choke holds on each other and punch.

Athletes sometimes died in this event! The match was over when one fighter was too hurt or tired to continue.

Athletes sometimes shaved their heads so their hair wouldn't get pulled.

Horse Racing

There were also horse-racing events at the Olympics. Crowds watched the races at a track called the *hippodrome* (HIP-poe-drome). *Hippos* is the Greek word for "horse."

97

The riders rode without saddles or stirrups.

Some races were for horseback riders. Others were for chariots pulled by teams of two or four horses or mules. Chariots were wooden carts driven by one man.

His job was dangerous . . . many drivers fell off! Not many chariots finished the race.

The winners of the horse races were not the drivers or riders. They were the owners. Women could own horses. This was the only Olympic sport women could actually win!

As many as 40 chariots stood at the starting line!

Girls actually had a separate festival during the Olympics. It was dedicated to Hera. Girls ran footraces that were a little shorter than the men's.

Closing Ceremonies

Winners were announced after each event. They got their prizes on the last day of the festival. People filled the stadium. The air was tense with excitement. The athletes marched in, decorated with purple ribbons.

Trumpets sounded. Heralds called out the names of the winners and their towns. The judges crowned each man with a sim-

100

ple *laurel* ~~olive~~ wreath. The leaves came from a special tree near the temple of Zeus.

That night, there were feasts and celebrations. The next day, everyone began the long journey home.

There was a myth that Zeus himself had planted the tree.

When the winners returned home, they were greeted like heroes. They brought fame and glory to their cities. They received wonderful gifts. Some athletes had statues of themselves placed in the agora. Others had poems written to celebrate their victories. Some athletes were given jobs and even free meals for life!

Turn the page to meet two very famous Olympic winners from ancient Greece.

Milo of Croton—the Wrestler

Milo of Croton won six Olympic victories.

He was so strong, he could bend nails between two fingers. It was said that once he even carried a cow on his shoulders!

There's a sad story about Milo's death. One day, he saw a tree in the woods with two iron wedges in it. Milo pulled the tree apart to get them. The trunk snapped back together, trapping his hands. He could not escape. That night, wild beasts of the forest ate him for dinner!

Diagoras of Rhodes—the Boxer

The Greeks thought Diagoras (die-uh-GOR-us) was the perfect athlete. No one else boxed with his skill, grace, or bravery.

When Diagoras was old, he visited the Olympics to see his sons compete. Both won. The sons lifted him onto their shoulders and carried him around the stadium.

Diagoras knew his life was complete. Bowing his head, he died peacefully in their arms.

8

The Olympics Today

After many wars, Greece lost its power. Other countries began to rule the land. The Olympic Games were no longer popular. They ended in AD 393. The ancient Olympic Games had lasted 1,170 years.

Even though the ancient Olympics ended, the Olympic spirit remained. Many years later, people decided to begin the Games again. The first modern Olympics took place in Greece in 1896.

Many things are different in the modern Olympics. The Games are no longer held to honor the gods. Today they are a sporting event only. They are not just held in Greece. Every Olympics, a different country hosts the Games. Athletes come from countries all over the world.

Today the Games are not just for men and boys. Women and girls play a big part in the Olympics. And today there are many more games. There are both summer and winter Olympics. The summer and winter Games are each held every four years.

Some things, however, are the same. Athletes still devote years to training. They still take an oath to compete fairly and to obey the rules. Like the ancient Greeks, they try to be good sports and to do their best.

The Winter Olympics include ice skating, skiing, and snowboarding.

Many events are still like those in the ancient Olympics. While there are no more chariots, there are events with horses. Athletes still run races and throw the javelin and the discus. There is still boxing, wrestling, and the long jump. There is even a pentathlon.

The modern Olympics are a spectacular sight. But the ancient Olympics were incredible, too. As the philosopher Epictetus (ep-ick-TEE-tus) wrote almost 2,000 years ago, "The Olympic Games are pretty uncomfortable. You are scorched by the sun and crushed by the crowds. You get soaked when it rains. You are deafened by the constant noise. But it's all worth it for the brilliant events you will see."

Doing More Research

There's a lot more you can learn about ancient Greece and the Olympics. The fun of research is seeing how many different sources you can explore.

Books

Most libraries and bookstores have lots of books about ancient Greece and the Olympics.

Here are some things to remember when you're using books for research:

1. You don't have to read the whole book. Check the table of contents and the index to find the topics you're interested in.

2. Write down the name of the book.
When you take notes, make sure you write down the name of the book in your notebook so you can find it again.

3. Never copy exactly from a book.
When you learn something new from a book, put it in your own words.

4. Make sure the book is <u>nonfiction</u>.
Some books tell make-believe stories about dolphins or sharks. Make-believe stories are called *fiction*. They're fun to read, but not good for research.

Research books have real facts and tell true stories. They are called *nonfiction*. A librarian or teacher can help you make sure the books you use for research are nonfiction.

Here are some good nonfiction books about ancient Greece and the Olympics:

- *Ancient Greece: A Guide to the Golden Age of Greece*, Sightseers series, by Julie Ferris and Julie Guerrero

- *Ancient Greece*, Find Out About series, by Richard Tames

- *Ancient Greece*, Journey into Civilization series, by Robert Nicholson

- *The Gods and Goddesses of Olympus* by Aliki

- *Growing Up in Ancient Greece* by Chris Chelepi

- *Science in Ancient Greece* by Kathlyn Gay

- *Spend the Day in Ancient Greece*, Spend the Day In series, by Linda Honan

Museums

Many museums have exhibits about ancient Greece. These exhibits can help you learn more about the ancient Greeks and the Olympics.

When you go to a museum:

1. Be sure to take your notebook!
Write down anything that catches your interest. Draw pictures, too!

2. Ask questions.
There are almost always people who can help you find what you're looking for.

3. Check the museum calendar.
Many museums have special events and activities just for kids!

Here are some museums around the country that have exhibits about ancient Greece:

- Brooklyn Museum of Art
  Brooklyn, New York

- Michael C. Carlos Museum
  Emory University, Atlanta, Georgia

- J. Paul Getty Museum
  Los Angeles, California

- Legion of Honor, Fine Arts Museums
  of San Francisco
  San Francisco, California

- The Metropolitan Museum of Art
  New York, New York

- North Carolina Museum of Art
  Raleigh, North Carolina

- University of Pennsylvania Museum of
  Archaeology and Anthropology
  Philadelphia, Pennsylvania

Videos

There are some great videos about ancient Greece. As with books, make sure the videos you watch for research are nonfiction!

Check your library or video store for these and other nonfiction videos about ancient Greece:

- *Ancient Greece* (Lost Treasures of the Ancient World series) from Kultur Video

- *Ancient Greece* from Schlessinger Media Company

- *Greek Gods* from A&E

- *Jim Henson's The Storyteller* (Greek Myths series) from Jim Henson Home Entertainment

- *Life, Times, and Wonders of Athens and Ancient Greece* from Questar Video, Inc.

115

The Internet

Many Web sites have lots of facts about Greece and the Olympics. Some also have games and activities that can help make learning about ancient Greece and the Olympics even more fun.

Ask your teacher or your parents to help you find more Web sites like these:

- www.bbc.co.uk/schools/ancientgreece/ athens/index.shtml

- www.gridclub.com/fact_gadget/the_greeks/ spotlight_on_ancient_greeks/the_olympic_ games/index.html

- www.historyforkids.org

- www.museum.upenn.edu

- www.perseus.tufts.edu

CD-ROMs

CD-ROMs often mix facts with fun activities.

Here are some CD-ROMs that will help you learn more about ancient Greece:

- *Ancient Greece*
  from Calvert School
- *The Road to Ancient Greece*
  from Ventura Educational Systems

Good luck!

Index

Photos courtesy of:

If you liked *Revolutionary War on Wednesday*, you'll love finding out the facts behind the fiction in

Magic Tree House® Research Guide

AMERICAN REVOLUTION

A nonfiction companion to *Revolutionary War on Wednesday*

It's Jack and Annie's very own guide to the American Revolution!

Look for it September 2004!

Magic Tree House® Books

Other books by Mary Pope Osborne:

Picture books:

The Brave Little Seamstress

Happy Birthday, America

Kate and the Beanstalk

Mo and His Friends

Moonhorse

New York's Bravest

Rocking Horse Christmas

First chapter books:

The *Magic Tree House®* series

For middle-grade readers:

Adaline Falling Star

After the Rain

American Tall Tales

The Deadly Power of Medusa by Mary Pope Osborne
    and Will Osborne

Favorite Greek Myths

Favorite Medieval Tales

Favorite Norse Myths

Jason and the Argonauts by Mary Pope Osborne
    and Will Osborne

The Life of Jesus in Masterpieces of Art
Mary Pope Osborne's Tales from <u>*The Odyssey*</u> series
Mermaid Tales from Around the World
My Brother's Keeper
My Secret War
One World, Many Religions
Spider Kane and the Mystery Under the May-Apple (#1)
Spider Kane and the Mystery at Jumbo Nightcrawler's (#2)
Standing in the Light
A Time to Dance by Will Osborne and
    Mary Pope Osborne

For young-adult readers:
Haunted Waters

MARY POPE OSBORNE and NATALIE POPE BOYCE are sisters who grew up on army posts all over the world. Today, Mary lives in New York City and Connecticut. Natalie makes her home nearby in the Berkshire Hills of Massachusetts. Mary is the author of over 50 books for children. She and Natalie are currently working together on *The Random House Book of Bible Stories* and on more Magic Tree House Research Guides.

Here's what Natalie and Mary have to say about working on *Ancient Greece and the Olympics:*

"We loved exploring the world of the ancient Greeks with Jack and Annie! We did a lot of research before we wrote the book. We always try to do some of it in museums. This time, we went to the University of Pennsylvania Museum of Archaeology and Anthropology. First, we met kids who were taking a summer workshop. They were learning all about ancient cultures. Then we wandered through the museum. We saw sculpture, pottery, and coins that the ancient Greeks actually used. Some of the pottery showed scenes of Greek life. One of the coins had the head of Athena on it. These things helped us imagine the way the Greeks lived. When we finished at the museum, we still wanted to learn more. This research could take a whole lifetime!"